D0070795

# The
# Black Hermit

Ngugi wa Thiong'o

# *The Black Hermit*

**HEINEMANN**

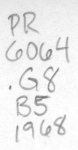

PR
6064
.G8
B5
1968

Heinemann is an imprint of Pearson Education Limited, a
company incorporated in England and Wales, having its registered
office at Edinburgh Gate, Harlow, Essex, CM20 2JE.
Registered company number: 872828

Heinemann is the registered trademark of
Pearson Education Limited

Heinemann Publishers (Pty) Limited
PO Box 781940, Sandton 2146, Johannesburg, South Africa

13-digit ISBN: 978 0 435900 51 9

Printed and bound in Great Britain by
Cox & Wyman Ltd, Reading, Berkshire

08   20

*For*
*Bethuel Kurutu*

# Preface

Drama in East Africa is mainly in the hands of the amateur.
The European amateur has tended to produce plays of little
appeal to Africans or, which is about the same thing, of
little relevance to conditions and problems in East Africa.
The African amateur was, and still is, to be found in schools
and universities: here however he tends to produce plays
with an eye on school certificate examinations. Thus in some
schools an annual production of Shakespeare with African
boys dressed in the costumes of Sixteenth century England,
has become — like Speech Day — a ritual.

One of the few groups trying to break away from this dry
convention is Makerere Students Dramatic Society. They
have produced Wole Soyinka, Brecht, and in 1966 they
set up a travelling company which toured many parts of
Uganda and Kenya — playing in village-halls, in churches
and in the open air.

They first came to life in 1961 when under Nathaniel
Frothingham (then an American student-scholar in Shakes-
peare) and Peter Kinyanjui (who had taken part in many
Shakespeare productions at Alliance High School in Kenya)

they produced *Macbeth* in a local setting. In 1962 Uganda became independent and the society wanted 'something original', a break with the past, for their own contribution to the Uhuru celebrations. *The Black Hermit*, first produced at the Uganda National Theatre in November 1962, was the child of that demand.

I thought then that tribalism was the biggest problem besetting the new East African countries. I, along with my fellow undergraduates, had much faith in the post-colonial governments. We thought they genuinely wanted to involve the masses in the work of reconstruction. After all, weren't the leaders themselves sons and daughters of peasants and workers? All the people had to do was to co-operate. All we had to do was to expose and root out the cantankerous effects of tribalism, racialism and religious factions.

I would like to thank many people – actors and producers – who helped this child to its feet. Bethual Kurutu, Peter Kinyanjui, Miss Gutzar Nensi, David Cook, and many others. I must especially mention Mrs. Kathy Sood, who, as the secretary to the production, several times went through the script with me. From the start to the eve of the dress rehearsal she and I were making alterations, all of which the over-worked actors took with an unusual patience.

James Ngugi

This play was first produced by The Makerere College Students Dramatic Society at the Uganda National Theatre in November, 1962, with the following cast:

| | |
|---|---|
| *Remi* | John Agard (Uganda) |
| *Omange* | Goody Godo (Malawi) |
| *Thoni* | Rhoda Kayanja (Uganda) |
| *Nyobi* | Suzie Oomen (India) |
| *Jane* | Celia Powell (Britain) |
| *Pastor* | Peter Kinyanjui (Kenya) |
| *Leader* | Bethuel Kurutu (Kenya) |
| *1st Elder* | Herman Lupogo (Tanzania) |
| *2nd Elder* | John Monyo (Tanzania) |
| *1st Neighbour* | George Ong'ute (Kenya) |
| *2nd Neighbour* | Frieda Kase (Uganda) |
| *Woman* | Lydia Lubwama (Uganda) |

# *Characters*

Remi            A clerk with an oil company.
                Formerly a student-cum-politician.
Omange          His friend in the City.
Thoni           His wife.
Nyobi           His mother.
Jane            His white girl-friend in the City.
Pastor          ⎫
Leader          ⎪
Elders          ⎪
1st Neighbour   ⎬ All from the village.
2nd Neighbour   ⎪
A woman         ⎪
A crowd         ⎭

# The
# Black Hermit

# ACT I
## The Country

### SCENE I

*A hut in the country. Thoni kneels on the floor near the hearth, sorting out beans spread in a basin. Enter Nyobi, a middle-aged woman, carrying a water-barrel which she puts down in a corner.*

NYOBI

Have you finished sorting out the beans?
Are they not yet ready to cook?

THONI

They are about ready, mother.

NYOBI

Aah,
You have again been crying
Letting the bitter water
Tear and wear your cheeks
To acquire a face like mine.

## ACT I

THONI

(*Turns head aside*)

NYOBI

(*To herself*)
Of a truth,
This world is really bad
Not the same as the old
When sons still gave respect to parents,
Honouring claims of motherhood,
Hearkening to the call of blood and soil.
Many letters have we now sent to him,
But no reply,
Not a word from him, a child I bore,
And like a plant in the field
Tended carefully,
Anxiously watching the sun, the wind and the rain,
That no malicious weather should come to harm him.
(*To Thoni*)
I, your mother in all ways but birth,
Am pained to see the gradual waste of your maidenhood.

THONI

Oh, mother.

NYOBI

Have you now,
In your heart alone,
Gone over what I told you?

THONI

How can I,
A woman without strength or learning hear it?

2

I cannot now go to a third husband.
I cannot roll from hand to hand,
A public ball, or a common whore,
Making myself cheap before the world.
Rather than that,
I shall die and have the grave for a bed.

NYOBI

Don't let such thoughts trouble you,
Poison your rest and peace.

THONI

Yet I can't do without a husband,
Without a man to warm my bed,
A man to ask me for a meal in the evening,
A man to make me wash his clothes;
And a child of my own,
A child to call me mother,
To make me feel a new self.

NYOBI

I am an old woman.
These eyes have seen the rain come and go,
Have seen sunrise and sunset,
Seasons followed by many others,
Birth and death alternating.
All these have taught me,
The lot of women will never change.
For you and me, Anjiru, Njene, Wihaki,
Independence has no meaning
Other than the one I knew yesterday:
I have tasted the pains of beating,

The pangs of birth and death's blows.
One lesson only have I learnt:
A woman's joy is scolding her children.
It lies in seeing their smiles and cries,
Doing little things for them, the loved ones.
A woman without a child is not a woman.
But I've also learned that
To be kicked and humiliated follows this joy
When the children grow.
Why has my son kept silent for so many years?
What are my tears to him?
What are my prayers?

### THONI

It's not you he hates,
It's my flesh and bed.

### NYOBI

I hate to see your youth wearing away,
Falling into bits like a cloth long hung in the sun!
Go and get another husband.
The world will not wait for you.
I tell you take a man.
If he does not marry you,
He may at least give you a child.

### THONI

Christ have mercy on me.
If this be a curse put upon me,
Remove it.
Why do men not rest in my hands?
Death took away my first husband.

Now the next, his brother, has left me.
The hut's gloom and loneliness
Has started eating into me.
Yet Christ,
Rid me of this thing,
This temptation harping on my weak flesh.
No, no, no.
I will not go with another,
But him I call my husband,
Even if I wait for twenty years and more,
I shall bear all.

NYOBI

Child.

THONI

Mother.

NYOBI

I fear for you.

THONI

Don't worry about me.
I am ashamed of my weakness.
Look now.
I'll not cry any more,
And when I feel grief come,
I'll go out and seek companions in the trees on the hills.
I'll watch little birds,
And lizards and insects.
Often at night,
I've walked about, alone,
Letting the moon and the stars speak to me.

# ACT I

At times, darkness shelters me.

NYOBI

Wait!
A thought comes into my mind.
Remi was once a God-fearing child,
Obedient to me and his father,
Always desiring to do the right thing.
I shall go to the pastor.
He knows our son is lost,
Swallowed by the pleasures of the city,
And to him I will say:
Go to the city, oh prophet of God,
Tell Remi to come back to us.
(*A voice is heard, outside the hut. They become excited*)
Who is that?

THONI

It might be Remi.

NYOBI

My son!

THONI

I shall not speak to him.

NYOBI

Hm! He shall know what I think of him.

THONI

I shall turn my back to him.
(*She stands with her back to the door. Enter an elder. Thoni and Nyobi are disappointed*)

ELDER

Is it well with you women of the house?

NYOBI

It is well.
Will you not sit down?
(*Thoni goes out*)

ELDER

Thank you wife of Ngome,
May God guard his spirit.
He was a man, oh yes your husband was,
Before the white-man stole his heart
And turned him into a Christian.
The Gods themselves are jealous,
They only take away the choicest in the land,
Leaving the weak and the feeble.

NYOBI

My heart is still heavy with grief.
I long ago feared that someone had put a curse on this
house.

My first son, so big and strong,
Was taken from me, like that,
For no reason that a man could divine.
And not a year had passed
Since he brought us joy
By marrying a young girl,
The best in the land.
Our tears had hardly dried
Before my man follows.
And now, Remi,
The only man left to head this house,
Went and died to us in the city.

## ACT I

ELDER

I came because of him.

NYOBI

Has he been found?

ELDER

We knew him once for a good son.
He acceded to our wishes
And married this woman,
A daughter of the tribe,
Instead of going to a white-skinned woman.
We were happy.
Remi was not the husband of Thoni, alone.
Remi was also the new husband to the tribe.
Through his big education,
He would have bound us together.
He should have formed a political party,
And led us to victory.
But we, like you, were puzzled.
Why did he go away from us?
Is that natural?
We, the ridge, the tribe, have waited.
We fear.

NYOBI

What?

ELDER

Shall I say it?

NYOBI

Speak quietly,
Or you tear my heart with false speculations.

8

**ELDER**

You know what our neighbours are.
The tribes that surround us
Don't want to see us rise.
Who knows?
You are there.
I, your neighbour, here
Can't I use black magic
To turn your mind against the tribe and this hearth?

**NYOBI**

Do you think so?

**ELDER**

Why not?
You have eyes and cannot see.
Remi, your son and ours,
Is the only educated man in all the land,
Exceeding in knowledge all the people,
Black and white put together.

**NYOBI**

Christo, save my son.
Make ineffective the bad medicine,
That turns away his mind from home.
Elder,
What shall I do?
Can't you and the tribe do something?

**ELDER**

I was sent to you by the elders.

**NYOBI**

What do they want?

## ACT I

**ELDER**

Your heart's wish.

**NYOBI**

My son?

**ELDER**

We want to send a man to the city,
A man who will carry a little medicine,
To make Remi turn to the tribe.

**NYOBI**

(*Suspicious*)
Who – who gave the medicine?

**ELDER**

Ha! Ha- Ha-!
We of Marua tribe are not children,
Or foolish, either.
Do you still believe in what the white-man said?
He said our medicine was bad, bad!
Some people were easily deceived,
And even now, four full years after Independence,
They have not discovered the lie.
You still call yourself a Christian?
I'll tell you.
Last month our diviner had a message from God.
He had a vision,
And there,
He saw the tribe expand,
Becoming powerful,
Dominating the whole country.
But here was a problem.

The tribe had first to tend a plant,
A green plant in their midst.
The green life would lead us to power and glory.

NYOBI

Where will you get the plant?

ELDER

Remi, Remi.
We must fetch him from the city.
We thought you had a message for him.

NYOBI

Tell him,
His wife and mother want him back.
Oh, Elder,
If you can make him —

ELDER

Trust Marua medicine to do its work.

NYOBI

I — I do.

ELDER

And —

NYOBI

Yes.

ELDER

There is something else.
We wanted you
To give our messengers and their medicine,
A mother's blessings,
To attend them on this difficult journey.

NYOBI

With all my heart.
Go in peace, and success attend you.
(*Elder goes out*)


NYOBI

What have I done?
I know Christo hates our medicine.
Suppose God punished me
So that Remi does not come back?
(*She looks for a shawl. Enter Thoni*)

THONI

Has the elder gone?

NYOBI

They're going to fetch him.

THONI

Remi.

NYOBI

Yes.

THONI

Oh, mother,
What are you doing?

NYOBI

Looking for my shawl.
I must see the pastor.
We must send him to the city.

THONI

But the elders are going —

NYOBI

I know.
It needs the power of Christ,
Together with power of the tribe,
To bring back Remi.

## SCENE II

*A meeting ground. In the open.*

LEADER

(*of the elders*) Elders of the tribe. I know you all want Remi to come back.

ELDERS

Yes. Remi must come back.

LEADER

I am not making a speech. But a word, one word I must share with you. We elders of Marua love our soil. Because we love that soil, we, years ago, agreed to fight the white-man and drive him away from the land. Today the same love of our soil makes us turn to the only educated man in the country. Look at our country since Independence. Where is the land? Where is the food? Where are the schools for our children? Who of our tribe is in the government? Who of our own flesh and blood can be seen in long cars and houses built of stone? Our tribe waits under a government composed of other tribes. What has Uhuru brought us?

ELDERS

Nothing.

LEADER

Not nothing. It has brought us heavier and heavier taxation. We are told about roads, about hospitals; but which hungry man wants a road? When we all stood solidly behind the Africanist Party we thought that once Uhuru was gained, taxation, for the poor, would stop.

ELDERS

Remi must come. Remi must save us.

LEADER

Be patient. When we went to the diviner, he asked us to choose three elders who would go to the city and, using the medicine he gave us, seduce Remi back to the tribe. Who can doubt that Remi's mind was spoilt by the evil eyes of our neighbours? The letters he wrote to us while he acquired knowledge at college and his speeches asking us to join the Africanist Party that's now in power, show that he could be a credit to the tribe – . Anyway, I have chosen the two elders who will go with me.

(*Enter an elder*)

ELDER

Peace to you, elders of the tribe.

LEADER

Did the woman pour blessing on our mission?

ELDER

Like rain. Her son is dearer to her than her Christianity.

LEADER

Turn we now our eyes to the mountain
And say, So be it, oh Creator.

**ELDERS**

So be it, oh Creator.

**LEADER**

So be it, oh great Creator.

**ELDERS**

So be it, thou shining Creator.

**LEADER**

The sun shall not be hotter than our medicine.

**ELDERS**

So be it, oh Creator.

**LEADER**

The wind shall not resist our medicine.

**ELDERS**

So be it, oh Creator.

**LEADER**

The mountains shall be moved by our medicine.

**ELDERS**

So be it, oh Creator.

**LEADER**

Remi shall come back to us.

**ELDERS**

So be it, oh Creator.

**LEADER**

No tribe shall be stronger than Marua.

**ELDERS**

So be it, oh Creator.

**LEADER**

So be it, oh great Creator.

**ALL**

So be it, ever and ever.

**LEADER**

One word more. When Remi comes back, he must not fall under the influence of his mother, or the pastor. You all know what a fine man his father was, before he came under their influence and lost all his manhood. He never became himself, except when he was near death. Then he turned to us, not his wife, to make Remi marry this woman. That should show you our strength. Let us now go. We shall again meet here, when —

**ALL**

Remi comes back.

# SCENE III

*The same.*
*Enter Pastor, Nyobi running after him.*

**NYOBI**

Pastor, Pastor.

**PASTOR**

Are you well with Christ?

**NYOBI**

I am coming to your house.
You must help us.

**PASTOR**

Rise my daughter.
Don't kneel before me, a mortal,

Else you invite the wrath of Christ,
Who long ago shed his blood
To wash our sins away.
But what's the trouble?
You look strained.
What load sits in your heart?

NYOBI

I've been caught.
The elders guiled me.

PASTOR

What do you mean?

NYOBI

It's my son.

PASTOR

Remi?
Has he come back?

NYOBI

No.
They want to send for him.
So they came to me for blessings
And I, overwhelmed by a mother's desire to see her son back,
Betrayed my heart,
Giving the required blessings.

PASTOR

Christ or Paul said that
Our loins should always be girt
With readiness
And our body, with armour.

# ACT I

What will happen when they bring him back?
He'll be lost to us,
And the shadow of Christ
Will not be there to cool him.
He was once a good son
Long before he went to this University.
He was then a good follower of Christ.
I remember how,
On days he would meet me
And running to me would say,
'Pastor, Pastor! Who died on the cross?'
I, glowing with hidden pride would ask him,
'Who?'
'I know!' he would presently say,
'Christ died on the tree!'
'For whom?'
'For me.'

NYOBI

Ah Remi!

PASTOR

When he went to this University —
Ah! I always said Satan was clever:
Involved him in politics
And other wordly pleasures and power —
He became — ah — well —
That Africanist Party: was he not a member?

NYOBI

He was,
God help him.

**PASTOR**

Politics.
He became lost to us.
Like a seed
Which falling on the wayside
Lacked the nourishment of the rich earth,
He dried up — was lost.

**NYOBI**

I want him back, Pastor.
Remi left a young wife.
And she, like a sapling in a drought-stricken land,
Will also dry up in the heat of desolation.

**PASTOR**

You must not think about the flesh.

**NYOBI**

She is young.
(*Pastor starts to move away. She runs after him calling, 'Pastor, Pastor'*)

**NYOBI**

She is a seedling
Whose eventual fruit
Will be a blessing to us all.
But a seedling needs a gardener.

**PASTOR**

Nyobi.

**NYOBI**

Yes.

**PASTOR**

You love Christ?

**NYOBI**

Yes.

**PASTOR**

Know you not what Christ has done for you?
Though your husband was called,
And also, your first son,
God has given you that child
So you may lead her to the cross.
Salvation is not achieved through the flesh.

**NYOBI**

It's hard for her.

**PASTOR**

Let us pray.
God of Abraham, God of Isaac,
Look down upon us.
We are not strong,
But you can save us.
Be with Nyobi.
Make her think of heaven
So she may bring that child
To love you and work for you.

**PASTOR and NYOBI**

Amen.

**NYOBI**

But —

**PASTOR**

Yes.

**NYOBI**

Remi.

PASTOR

What?

NYOBI

Pray for him also.

PASTOR

I'll open my mind to you.
Your son went away,
Was lured by Satan into the City.
At college, he became wayward,
Digressed from the paths of holiness.
God wanted him for a sower of Christ's seeds.
Why else did God give him that education?
To lead many a lost sheep,
Back to Christ, his master. But
Remi refused to go to Nineveh,
He fled to the City of idolatry.

NYOBI

So God help him.

PASTOR

Go home now.
Look to the child.
Bring her up to fear God.
God will forgive you.

NYOBI

Pastor.

PASTOR

Yes.

NYOBI

Will you not go?

# ACT I

**PASTOR**

Where?

**NYOBI**

To the City.

**PASTOR**

The City!

**NYOBI**

Yes. Go. Go there.
Bring back our son.
He'll listen to you.
I need him.

**PASTOR**

(*Thoughtful*) Maybe we Christians need him too.
I am old.
My day's end is near.
And now that Uhuru has come,
Bringing new problems,
Christ's Church will need young blood.

**NYOBI**

Too true, God be thanked.

**PASTOR**

I will go to the City.

# ACT II
## *The City*

### SCENE I

*Opens in a street-corner. A group of young people of different races playing the guitar and jiving suggests the atmosphere of a dance-club. The rest of the stage is in darkness. Intense and close at first, the music soon fades into the distance. The scene suddenly changes to Remi's room. Remi is lying on a sofa. Enter Jane.*

JANE

Hello Remi.

REMI

Oh Jane, it's lovely to see you.

JANE

What! Aren't you ready yet? Just like you to wait to the last minute.

REMI

Oh I'm sorry, I just suddenly felt tired, not equal to a night out.

JANE

(*Laughs*)

REMI

What's the matter?

JANE

(*Continues laughing*)

REMI

What's the matter? Are you possessed?

JANE

Wonderful, wonderful, superb.

REMI

What the —

JANE

Imagine you saying you are tired. It's enough to make anyone split their sides.

REMI

No, seriously, I'm tired.

JANE

Would you have said that last year? You went from night-club to night-club as if you were haunted, running away from something.

REMI

Jane!

JANE

Yes?

REMI

You must not say that.

24

JANE

Why?

REMI

Perhaps, well, perhaps I was haunted.

JANE

What do you mean?

REMI

Oh nothing.

JANE

Tell me what's the matter with you Remi. You have changed so much over the last few weeks, always brooding over something and your eyes fixed in space. Tell me all. I may be able to help you.

REMI

You know, you remind me of my mother — always over-anxious about the well-being of her children. Remi, my child, you look tired to-day. You are not eating your food. Remi, what is worrying you? What did they do to you in school? Perhaps I may be able to help you —

JANE

Don't be so sarcastic. Come, tell me about your mother. You are always so silent about your family.

REMI

She is old, goes to the river for water, to the forest for firewood — and of course she worries over me. What else?

JANE

What does she think of her educated son?

REMI

The usual things — wanted me to marry and have a home

and children. But you see, I used to be so shy with girls—

JANE

You! Shy with girls! And you almost ate me the very day you met me in the club! How is it that our dear, little, shy boy learnt dancing and to be so bold with women, even those who are strangers to him?

(*Remi does not respond*)

Something is worrying you. Ah, I know what it is. Don't you want to take me out? You don't have to, you know.

REMI

(*Shakes his head*)

JANE

No? Then it's about home. Why don't we go there. I mean home to your parents?

REMI

Why don't I go home?

JANE

Remember you have never taken me there?

REMI

Jane?

JANE

Yes.

REMI

One day you'll know. It's only that I'm tired of this city — that's all. I hate working for these oil-companies that have invaded our country. Files, files, files all day long.

JANE

Go home. Become a teacher. That's creative isn't it?

REMI

And starve — while ministers and their permanent secretaries fatten on bribes and inflated salaries.

JANE

Many of your people would be glad to earn your teacher's salary.

REMI

True — but — . Anyway, let's stop talking about these things. They say life is too short. Shall we go?

JANE

To the night club?

REMI

Yes.

JANE

You're so sweet!
(*They embrace*)

## SCENE II

*Same room. The following day. Remi is alone reading a Sunday paper. Suddenly there's loud, rough knocking at the door.*

REMI

Come in.
(*More knocking. Rather insolent*)
Come in — whoever you are.
(*Enter Omange — laughing. Remi pretends to be angry*)
You rogue.

27

OMANGE

(*Exaggerated politeness*) I believe we have met before. Are you Mr. – eh – Mr. –

REMI

I will kill you, you bastard!

OMANGE

Oh – Mr. Kill me. (*They both start laughing*) Hello.

REMI

Hello. You can sit on the chair, the table, the floor, – or go out.

OMANGE

How was the night?

REMI

A bit of waltzing, a bit of rocking, and plenty of twisting and cha cha cha. You know – the usual stuff. By the way, have you seen this? (*Shows Omange the Sunday paper. Omange reads it*)

OMANGE

You know Remi, I fear for our country. Independence has not reduced the amount of racial tension. This affair of an Asian girl who has been ostracised by her community because she was seen going round with an African is not an isolated case.

REMI

You were ever optimistic and would not believe in the government legislating on social matters.

OMANGE

You didn't get my point. It depends on what kind of government, on the kind of legislation and on the kind of issues.

28

REMI

Depends, depends! Depends on the kind of kind of what!

OMANGE

You may mock me. But take tribalism for instance. Since Independence tribalism and tribal loyalties seem to have increased. And even leaders who were the supporters of the Africanist Party are the very ones who are encouraging these feelings. Do you think these people would pass an effective piece of legislation when it would touch the very taproot of their power?

REMI

Yes, some of these leaders were paying lip service, only lip service to the Africanist Party. But what do you think the government ought to do? Just preach sermons?

OMANGE

The government should act. It must deal firmly with anyone who is found exploiting racial, tribal or religious differences. But let us also remember that even a black man's government can go wrong. Take this legislation against strikes, for example.

REMI

If the government makes all strikes illegal, that will be the finest thing they have done so far. A government in a newly independent country can never be too firm.

OMANGE

But why wrench from a workman his only tool! A Trade Union without the right to strike is like a lion without claws and teeth. Tell me. Will the government also take over the land, the banks and oil companies and give them to our people? In any case, there are other ways of dealing with people who oppose you besides refusing to listen to them and crushing them.

REMI

What, for instance?

OMANGE

You could give them what they want, what they fought for. The manpower of the masses ought to be the cornerstone of our economy, not foreign aid.

REMI

You are like any of those politicians who oppose the government. They don't realise that the problems posed by Independence are different from those of colonial days. Then, of course, you could go on being destructive, for as a nationalist revolutionary your aim was to discredit the colonial power in the eyes of the people.

OMANGE

But people have a right to destroy a government, any government that continues the practice of the colonial régime.

REMI

Yes — but can't we outgrow the opposition mentality and help to build? Some people feel that they must go on opposing the government at every point. And it is more terrible when the opposition — like that of the Democratic Union — is based simply on tribe and religion. I hate this. Even at college I hated the many small political and social organisations based on tribe and race.

OMANGE

Of course I'd forgotten you took active part in national politics even at college.

REMI

Yes. I had the misfortune of being the first in my tribe to reach University. You know it's a small tribe. Elders listened to my voice. I wrote them letters, virtually ordering them to support the Africanist Party and our Prime Minister. And during vacations I held meetings everywhere and told them: Join the Africanist Party.

OMANGE

Why then didn't you stand for election? You had a good chance and maybe now you would be in the government.

REMI

I did not want to.

OMANGE

Why?

REMI

Because I was trapped by the tribe.

OMANGE

What do you mean?

REMI

I was caught. And when I realised this, it was too late for me to do anything about it.

OMANGE

What do you mean? You have never told me about this.

REMI

So I ran away, escaped to the city.

## ACT II

OMANGE

Don't be mystical!

REMI

I wanted to be myself.

OMANGE

Hm. By quiting politics — leaving it to tribalists and corrupt men? You're strange.

REMI

Not strange. It's a wound here. There are some wounds, Omange which can never be healed. Never!

OMANGE

I am sorry.

REMI

Perhaps I should have told you earlier. A friend might have helped me. My wound is a woman. You shake your head? But listen to me, Omange. I had a brother once. He was close to me. But in many ways he was different from me. He was stronger. He was a man of action. But me, I was shy with people. Women frightened me. A crowd was different though. I was all right standing before such a faceless thing. There was a girl in my village whom I secretly adored. But I was a dumb sufferer. Every day I thought I would declare my love. She never gave me a chance. Always looked at me with sharp eyes — bashful yet challenging. I tried to confide in my brother. But somehow something always prevented me. Then I went to college. One day I made up my mind. I would tell her. I would claim her. I was excited and in high spirits. The same day I had a letter from home—

OMANGE

Yes?

REMI

Well, she and my brother were to be married.

OMANGE

Married?

REMI

Yes. For a day or two I could only lie in bed. I thought that she and my brother had betrayed me. Couldn't they read my heart? Then I reasoned thus. She *must* have loved my brother all along. I was now calm. I thanked God that I had revealed nothing to either. At the end of the year I decided to go home. The girl no longer meant anything to me. In my mind she was my brother's wife. Yet — Do you ever have a premonition?

OMANGE

What?

REMI

Oh, that something is going to happen to you.

OMANGE

Sometimes. Why?

REMI

I remember that journey. I trembled all over without cause. I could hardly move. Suddenly I became sick. My friends in the train had to carry me home. Then — oh, how shall I put it?

OMANGE

Go on.

**REMI**

My brother was dead. Crushed by a motor-car. (*Pause*)
It's all over now. But then it was horrible – very horrible –
He had hardly been with his wife for more than six months.

**OMANGE**

What became of her?

**REMI**

Soon after this, my father fell ill. It was the shock of my
brother's death. He called me to his bed and said: 'Remi.
You know our custom. Your brother's wife is now your
wife.' I refused to marry her.

**OMANGE**

But you loved her?

**REMI**

Can't you see? I had already reconciled myself to the fact
that she was my brother's wife. And she was. How then
could I take another man's wife? I wanted a woman of my
own. But if I married this girl, how could I ever get it out
of my head that she belonged to another? Could I see her
as my wife? No. No. It is not that I am very religious. Even
today, I could run away with your wife if I knew she loved
me.

**OMANGE**

What happened?

**REMI**

O, my mother wept. My father, although a Christian,
wailed and cursed. The elders of the tribe came and prayed
me to do a father's wish and obey a sacred custom. Here
were people I was leading. I had asked them to be true and

faithful to the Africanist Party. They had obeyed me. Now they were asking me to show similar obedience. Finally I agreed to live with her.

OMANGE

You married her?

REMI

Yes.

OMANGE

Did she want to marry you?

REMI

Marry me? The girl never loved me.

OMANGE

How do you know? Did you ask her?

REMI

No!

OMANGE

Did you let her know that you loved her?

REMI

I knew she did not love me. Or she would not have married my brother. How could I go to her and say: Thoni, I love you, I have always loved you. Even if she had accepted and gave me some sort of love in return I would have known that she had turned to me to fill the emptiness in her heart, to soothe her grief for her true husband. Would you like to feel that a woman was using you because she couldn't have the man she really wanted?

OMANGE

Remi, I think you had better give up a mere clerk's job in an oil-company. Go home.

### REMI

Never. I shall not go home. I will never go home.

(*Enter leader with two other elders. Silence*) (*Agitated. To Omange*)

Please go. Jane and I were going out. Stop her. She must not come. These are elders from Marua.

(*Omange goes out*)

Is it well with you elders of the tribe?

### LEADER

Peace be with you.

### REMI

Is there anything the matter with the land? Or why do you wear such strain on your faces? And you drop down your heads as if something weighty sits in your hearts? You make me afraid when you turn your eyes from me so.

### ELDERS

(*Silence*)

### REMI

Speak now. Your silence touches my heart. It forbodes no good.

### LEADER

You left us.

### 1ST ELDER

We no longer see your shadow.

### 2ND ELDER

We have nowhere to rest.

### REMI

Fathers of the tribe. These things had to be. It was my fault in more ways than one. Let that be the end. If it

is the old swelling about representing you in government,
I cannot, even now, change my mind.

LEADER

We love the soil.

REMI

I too loved the soil.

1ST ELDER

We love the tribe.

2ND ELDER

We want to serve the tribe.

REMI

I too loved and served the tribe.

LEADER

We followed you and fought the white-man.

REMI

I fought the white-man and followed you.

1ST ELDER

Our tribe wails under the new government.

2ND ELDER

No son of our soil is a D.O.

LEADER

Not one of our skin and blood
Is in the new government.

REMI

What do you want?

1ST ELDER

Son of Ngome
You long ago

37

Asked us, your tribe,
To support the Africanist Party.

                    2ND ELDER
And promised us freedom.

                    REMI
You have your freedom.

                    LEADER
Taxation.

                    1ST ELDER
Forced community work.

                    2ND ELDER
The drought in the land.

                    LEADER
Our crops have failed.

                    1ST ELDER
Our animals no longer give us milk.

                    2ND ELDER
And no jobs for those of our tribe.

                    REMI
We are all black.

                    LEADER
Yes –
When we fought the white-man
But now –

                    1ST ELDER
My son is my son.

                    2ND ELDER
My village my village.

LEADER

My tribe still my tribe.
You must help us.

1ST and 2ND ELDER

You must lead us.

LEADER

You must save us.

ALL

You must save us.

LEADER

Fathers need you at home.

1ST ELDER

And mothers cry for you.

2ND ELDER

The tribe waits for you.

REMI

But stop!

LEADER

We want a tribal political party.

1ST ELDER

A Prime Minister from the tribe.

2ND ELDER

A husband to all the land.

REMI

Wait!
(*Walks about pensively*)
What do you want with me?

LEADER

First come home.

## ACT II

1ST ELDER

Go to the new D.O.

2ND ELDER

Your word will carry weight.

LEADER

Tell him of our afflicted land.

1ST ELDER

And all our other troubles.

2ND ELDER

No more taxation.

ALL

The white-man has gone.

LEADER

A D.O. from the tribe.
We ask no more than your leadership.

REMI

You want me to come back home?

ALL

We do.

REMI

You really want me to lead you?

ALL

We do.

REMI

Then, all of you, go home. I will never, never come back.

LEADER

We go.

1ST ELDER

We leave you.

40

**2ND ELDER**

Our son.

**LEADER**

But we know in our hearts,
You will not fail us.
(*As they go out, one elder drops down a small bundle, well-wrapped with dry banana leaves*)

**REMI**

Never! Never!
Has our nationalist fervour that gave us faith and hope in days of suffering and colonial slavery been torn to shreds by such tribal loyalties? All my life I believed in the creation of a nation. Where are we now? Perhaps I did wrong to come to the city following the inclination of my heart. Yet how can I go home? Surely a man's public life is given meaning only by the stability of his private life.
(*Enter Pastor. Silence*)
Oh! Good day, Pastor.

**PASTOR**

It is well.

**REMI**

You have come a long way.

**PASTOR**

It's not a long way
To a man's heart's desire,
And Christ is there to lead the way.

**REMI**

The land and the people, all right?

### PASTOR

We need you. No, God needs you.

### REMI

Even you, Pastor? You want a political party?

### PASTOR

Not so, my child.
Your mother needs you.

### REMI

She has no needs.

### PASTOR

She daily grows weak,
Do you want her to die?

### REMI

It's her own affair.

### PASTOR

Remember that
She gave birth to you.

### REMI

Yes — she's my mother.

### PASTOR

She gave you milk when
You were young and weak
Not knowing yourself.

### REMI

(*Silent*)

### PASTOR

Save her.

### REMI

I am not a saviour.

42

PASTOR

It's a Christian duty to save.

REMI

I have no life to save.

PASTOR

The children of God want you.
And Christ calls you to lead them to the Cross.

REMI

Do the people of God want me to be a priest? Ha! Ha!

PASTOR

It's the voice of God.

REMI

I will not come home.

PASTOR

Then we sink.

REMI

No cause for that.

PASTOR

You once loved the gospel.
God made you the only one,
With education and understanding,
Born of a widened horizon.
For nothing?
Your learning is not your learning,
It's for all the people

REMI

Pastor, you want me back in the village? To serve mother?

PASTOR

Your mother,

43

And all other Christians.

REMI

I once served mother,
Acceding to her wishes
That day she clung to me,
Asking me to — to —
Oh, oh,
Why, you, pastor,
Why should you remind me ....
(*Pensive. Silence. Then Remi turns to the Pastor with an
ironic smile*)
Pastor.
Go.
Go back to the village.
Tell the elders this:
If they need me, I'll come.
If you Christians want me, I'll not fail you.
If my mother calls for me,
I'll not again disappoint her hopes.
Go and tell it to all:
The ridges, hills and the mountains,
Tell it to all the land.

PASTOR

God bless you my child.
(*Pastor goes out and leaves a bible behind*)

REMI

I have been too long a hermit
In the City.
I'd thought I'd escape

From things that were me —
That were part of my life.
I must now rise and go to the country.
For I must serve our people,
Save them from traditions and bad customs,
Free them from tribal manacles.
Now.
(*Then he sees the bible, takes it, and also the small bundle left by the elders. He weighs them in both hands. He is clearly moved*)
These — These —
Pieces of superstition
Meant to lure me home.
Shall I find my peace and freedom there?
These are part of me,
Part of my life,
My whole life.

## SCENE III

*The same, a few days later.*

                    JANE
You are still determined to go?
                    REMI
Yes.
                    JANE
You are going to leave me.
                    REMI
Yes.

JANE

But how can you?

REMI

The nation calls.

JANE

What is this nation?

REMI

Me, you, people.

JANE

Oh, what shall I do? You are so callous. You've no feelings.

REMI

My tribe calls. I no longer want to be a hermit in the city.

JANE

A hermit?

REMI

I came here in search of solitude.

JANE

In night-clubs and wild parties?

REMI

Seclusion from what was formerly around you is solitude.
To be a hermit means escaping from what's around you.
My tribe was around me.

JANE

And now you are going back? The tribe calls you from your
solitude. Tell me Remi: what's the tribe?

REMI

I don't know.

JANE

Ah Remi, can't you remember all the sweet hours we had

together? Please take me with you. Don't leave me here alone. I too am a citizen of this country. I too can live with your tribe and be like the other women of the land.

REMI

You are different.

JANE

Because I work in an office? Typing and typing all day long? What do you mean, different?

REMI

You are different from me, from us, from the tribe. You cannot know what I know. Oh, I know your father was not a settler, is a teacher, one of the good sort. Still you have not experienced what I have experienced. Your background is a world from mine. How can we be the same? How can the call of the tribe be your call? To you tribalism and colonialism, the tyranny of the tribe and the settler are an abstraction. To me they are real. I have felt their shaft here. Yes, they have made a wound here, a wound that made me run to the city. To you, African nationalism and what it means to us who suffered under colonial rule for sixty years can only be an intellectual abstraction. But to me, my whole being — I am involved in it.

JANE

You? Do you honestly believe that race matters, that the colour of my skin or yours should form a barrier between people?

REMI

It's not the colour. It is just what you are, what I am.

*47*

JANE

My father left South Africa because he could not bear a racial regime. For all people are the same everywhere. What matters is not race, creed, or custom, but whether individuals can meet and understand one another. Just now you are betraying the ideals you used to mirror before my eyes. Hm. And you criticise Verwoerd!

REMI

When I came to the city running away from the tribe, I never knew I would ever go back. I wanted to be a hermit for ever. But now they have called me back. And I must go.

JANE

Remi: who are *they*?

REMI

My mother — all.

JANE

I don't understand.

REMI

You see, I told you. You can't understand. I don't want you to understand.

JANE

I can. I want to.

REMI

Don't seek to know any more about me and my past.

JANE

Tell me about your life. I've all along felt that there was something in your life that was hidden from me.

REMI

Jane.

JANE

Yes.

REMI

Don't make it hard for me.

JANE

Don't you love me?

REMI

I don't know what love is. Oh, I don't know. Maybe I like you. In fact I like you very much.

JANE

Only that? But you one day said you would marry me.

REMI

I then did not know my past would follow me. I'd thought I would die a hermit in the city.

JANE

What made you come into the city?

REMI

(*Silence*)

JANE

Tell me. Tell me this: what made you come to the city and heap lies on me?

REMI

I thought I would marry you. Maybe if I come back —

JANE

Why can't you take me with you? I'll be faithful to you and your people. I don't really like the city. I've always wanted to breathe the air in the mountains and feel the bite of the cold wind, the smell of the wild flowers and the deep darkness there.

REMI

Please go from me. Go now.

JANE

Why?

REMI

Just go.

JANE

I must know.

REMI

You insist? I had thought to spare you the pain.

JANE

Spare me nothing.

REMI

I am — I am married.

JANE

(*Stunned cold*)
Married? Did you say you were married?

REMI

Yes.

JANE

For how long?

REMI

I was married when we met.

JANE

But why didn't you tell me right at the beginning?

REMI

There was no need.

JANE

No need? When you knew I loved you?

REMI

But that was later, Jane. At first we were just friends, my life had nothing to do with yours. And then, when I knew you better — for I remember, you were so gay, and so wonderful — you made me forget my past, I needed you so much, I couldn't bear to tell you something that might make you leave me.

JANE

But didn't you think it might upset me just a little when I found out? (*Remi silent*) You said you would marry me You promised to marry me. Oh, promises, promises. I should have known what promises mean to you. You are like one of your precious politicians — they stand on a platform in front of the silly crowd and they shout, Give me your vote, and I'll give you shoes! You said to me, Give me your love, and I will marry you. But when the time comes, when you've got all you want, no shoes, no shoes!

REMI

Jane, you've got it all wrong. It wasn't like that at all. Time and time again I tried to tell you, but somehow I couldn't. I — I just couldn't bring myself to hurt you.

JANE

Hurt me? If you had told me at the beginning, it would not have hurt very much. I would have forgotten the pain. And now because of your waiting — And you talk of hurting!

REMI

Jane . . .

JANE

You call yourself a hermit. A black hermit. You are not a

hermit. A hermit looks for the truth. You ran away from the truth of your position. Tell me, why did you run away from your wife?

REMI

It wasn't a real marriage.

JANE

Why not?

REMI

She was my brother's widow. I had to marry her. It is a sacred custom of Marua Tribe.

JANE

But I thought you were against such primitive things.

REMI

The tribe had reared me. Given me education. They had followed me. How could I bring myself to hurt them? I obeyed them.

JANE

Why didn't you stay with them? Why did you run away?

REMI

I don't know. Oh, Jane, I don't know.

JANE

Yes, perhaps I am different from you. I know what I want, what I am. You don't know yourself, or what you really want. Only that you like thinking yourself a delicate being, superior and so much better than anybody else.

REMI

I never said that.

JANE

But you are weak, aren't you. Too weak to tell me the truth.

52

REMI

Please, Jane, listen to me.

JANE

Don't touch me. Go back to your tribe. Go back to your little wife. (*Runs out*)

REMI

(*After her*) Jane! Jane!

# ACT III

## *The Return of the Hermit*

### SCENE I

(*Nyobi and Thoni in the hut, tidying*)

NYOBI

The pastor said —
The pastor said Remi would come to-day.

THONI

Yes.

NYOBI

Why do you look so
With eyes downcast,
Betraying a sad heart?

THONI

I am happy
My heart is thankful

54

For many little and big things
You have done to me.
When Remi comes home
We shall ever live united.
And yet –

NYOBI

Yet –

THONI

I fear –

NYOBI

What?

THONI

He might be different.

NYOBI

No my child.
He'll be the same seed, which,
Nourished in rich soil,
Will grow to feed us all.

THONI

I don't know but,
Though I feel that
Here I must be joyful
Yet – oh – How shall I put it?
I have no fitting words
To clothe my thought.
Don't worry about me.
You wait and see – just see
How changed I shall be when
Remi, my husband, comes home to me.

#### NYOBI

You make me cold
When I hear you speak in that way,
Putting puzzled stops in your speech,
As if something weighty is still in your breast.

#### THONI

It's nothing.

#### NYOBI

Nothing?

#### THONI

It is here.

#### NYOBI

In your heart?

#### THONI

Yes.

#### NYOBI

You are still afraid.

#### THONI

I do want to be happy.
Christo has been good to us.
See, see, how blessed our lives are,
Since Remi said he would come,
Rain has fallen,
Putting an end to the anxious looks,
On the faces of us all.
The drought,
That threatened our lives,
Now seems over.

**NYOBI**

It is the way of God.

**THONI**

I feel not at ease.

**NYOBI**

Let not these things eat into you.

**THONI**

Last night I had a dream.
I saw a man
With the face of an Irimu . . .
What is it mother?
You look alarmed.

**NYOBI**

I too had such a dream.
(*Enter Pastor*)

**PASTOR**

Peace be unto this house.

**NYOBI**

Our hearts echo your words.
We feared you would not come,
To share with us this moment of gladness.

**PASTOR**

Remi is a chosen vessel of God.
I knew this once long ago
When Remi came to my Sunday School.
He would listen to me attentively.
My heart was filled with great joy

To see the young soul
So hearken to the small voice of God.
Again meeting in the big city,
I saw the same child,
Listening (oh how my heart leapt)
To the small voice.

NYOBI

O Pastor.
My cup runneth over.

PASTOR

It's not my work.
This is the work of Christ,
In the hearts of us all.
True Independence comes with Christ.

NYOBI

Will he really come to-day?

PASTOR

Doubt not.
But be prepared.
He must be kept away from politics,
Away from the influences of tribal elders.

NYOBI

You told the elders.

PASTOR

They had been to the city before me.
And I promised Remi I would tell them all.
With Christ nothing is hard.
Let us bow our heads in prayer.
(*As they bend their heads, a man comes running into the hut*)

### 1ST NEIGHBOUR

Nyobi! Thoni! Pastor.

### NYOBI

What is it?

### 1ST NEIGHBOUR

The elders meet.
So many of them.
People 've come from afar,
From ridges around and beyond
They pour into the meeting ground.
They dance and sing.
Hark!
You can hear the drums.
They carry branches.
And sing old songs of war
When we, Marua, used to be a tribe,
Before the white-man came.
Now they sing of another coming,
After the going of the white-man.
They sing of a new man,
To restore the tribe to its land,
To its old ways.
No more taxation.
There will be freedom.

### PASTOR

Who is the saviour they sing about?
They must not blaspheme.

## ACT III

Let us pray.

Who is he?

Your son.
He'll come to-day.
To lead us back to glory.
Oh hear them.
They come nearer.
Not going to the meeting ground?
Tell me,
Is it true Remi comes home to-day?
Oh there they are.
So many.
I must go. (*goes out*)

**PASTOR**

Let us now pray.

**NYOBI**

The drums call.
Must I not be there when he comes?

**PASTOR**

Don't mix with them.

**NYOBI**

Remi is my son.

**PASTOR**

Remi is the son of Christ.

**NYOBI**

Thoni,

*60*

Are you coming?

                    THONI

I fear.
Let me come later,
When I have prayed to my God.
(*Nyobi goes out*)
Don't leave me Pastor.

                    PASTOR

I am not going, child.

                    THONI

Pray for us pastor.
Do you think Remi will come?

                    PASTOR

God will guide him home.

                    THONI

Listen.
(*Runs to the door*)
I hear some noise.
They shout. They cheer.
Pastor! Pastor!
It is him.
It is him.

                    PASTOR

Don't be so excited.
He'll come home to you.

                    THONI

But I know he has come.
I must go.
I must hear him speak.

# ACT III

**PASTOR**

Wait —
(*Another person comes running in*)

**THONI and PASTOR**

What is it?

**2ND NEIGHBOUR**

All the tribe.

**THONI**

Has he arrived?

**2ND NEIGHBOUR**

Didn't you hear the roar?
I could not bear it.

**PASTOR**

What? The roar?

**2ND NEIGHBOUR**

His voice.
He was angry.
He was not alone.
He was with a man from another tribe.
He made him stand on the platform,
And linking hands with him, said:
This is a man from Njobe tribe.
He is my brother and yours.
You should have been there,
How he blamed the elders,
The Leader and the others,

62

For preaching tribalism,
Misleading us all.
Our salvation lay in the National Party.
People were then quiet.
Some turned their heads away
Stung by his wrathful words.
Other elders went away in guilt and shame.
Eh, what is that?
(*They run to the door. Singing voices can be heard, becoming louder and louder*)
It's Remi.
People crowd around him.
He comes here.
Now they sing
The National Anthem.
Let us join them.
(*They go out. Now the singing is quite loud.*
*The scene changes to the village square just outside Nyobi's hut. The crowd is singing Africa's anthem*:
Mungu Ibariki Afrika
Ili ipate Kuamka,
Maombi yetu yazikize
Uje,
Utubariki.
　Uje roho
　Uje roho
　Takatifu
　Uje leo
　Utubariki

# ACT III

*Thoni and the Pastor enter during the singing. They can just be seen at one end of the crowd. There is so much excitement that nobody notices them)*

REMI

Go now dear elders. And remember what I told you. We must all turn to the soil. We must help ourselves; build more schools; turn our hearts and minds to create a nation, then will tribe and race disappear. And man shall be free. . . . *(They all cheer wildly as they stream out. Now only Nyobi, Thoni, Pastor, Omange and Remi are left on the stage)*

REMI

Even you, pastor. You and other Christians must not live isolated. We must link hands, build a house in which you and I and all our people can live in peace, cultivating the riches of the heart.

PASTOR

God bless you and our country.

NYOBI

My son.

REMI

And you mother. I turn to you. What did you do to me? You harped on my weakness and made me marry a woman whose love and loyalty will ever lie with those in the grave.

NYOBI

You talk to me so? You talk to me so?

REMI

Everything will give way to my leadership.

**NYOBI**

My son, don't be dazzled by the blaze
Which will burn for a night and tomorrow it is out,
All ashes and blackness,
Look to your House:
And there you will see the fire that glows all night
and day, between three hearthstones.
There is food and the warmth of life waiting for you.

**PASTOR**

Listen to your mother,
And don't be hard on the woman,
She has waited for you,
Bearing all the ills of the land.

**REMI**

I will no longer be led by woman, priest or tribe. I'll crush
tribalism beneath by feet, and all the shackles of custom.
I was wrong to marry her who was another's wife, a woman
who did not love me.

(*Thoni goes out. Nobody notices her disappearance*)

**NYOBI**

Everything is not tribe and custom.
Your mother, your wife or child are not merely tribe.
Search your heart.
You have never known her.

**REMI**

I now know all. My stay in the city has taught me everything.

**PASTOR**

Our son —

NYOBI

Your words and face
Make fear creep in my flesh.
Where's Thoni?

PASTOR

Gone away.

NYOBI

I must go to her. (*Goes out*)

PASTOR

I will pray for her. (*Goes out*)

REMI

I don't want to see her.


# SCENE II

*The Same.*
*Enter Thoni running – followed by a village woman.*

WOMAN

Listen, child.

THONI

I can't stay here in this place.
To be like an unwanted maize plant
That has been pulled out and flung on the bare path.
To be trodden beneath men's feet,
And left to wither and dry up in the sun.

WOMAN

You must not go away.

THONI

Can't go back to a house of shame and humiliation,
To be laughed at, to be flouted,
To be driven out, and by him, my husband,
When I'd wanted to give him my body, my heart to keep.

WOMAN

He may change his mind.

THONI

I could not go back to him,
Even if he called me back.

WOMAN

Thoni.

THONI

See, see
I am not afraid.
I'll go through the world
A maid flouted by both fate and man.
And I'll go to a country where I've many times thought
of going.
There, there is no light and no people.
It's all darkness, swallowing you wholly
So no man from this world may know or recognise you.
I'll go there, I shall never meet anyone
Who'll see me and pause to whisper:
There is a girl no man will touch.
There is stillness, all stillness in that country
Which I saw only once when I was a child.
I was then small — very small.

**WOMAN**

God above protect us.

**THONI**

I felt pain here and I think that I cried.

My mother was worried and wept.

Then the light from the sun

Blinded me. I was in that country.

You think my mind is raving. But it is true.

The pain stopped. I could not see my father or my mother.

And I didn't want to see them.

It was so dark there and so quiet,

And the only song and talk was that of deep darkness.

A darkness that showed nothing of pain, laughter or suffering.

But peace . . . peace . . .

When I returned from the country

They said I had been dead

And only God's grace had brought me back to life.

But what a life!

**WOMAN**

You must not let your mind wonder so.

Come and stay with me.

Remi is not the only tree

Under whose shadow you can rest.

**THONI**

You don't know, you don't know.

Goodbye mother, goodbye father, goodbye my village.

And now I must go for darkness calls.

(*Goes out*)

## WOMAN

She was ever a strange woman,
Unknown to us who have been with her for so long.
But I must follow
And turn her distracted mind the right way.
Yet I fear,
I fear for her and for Nyobi
I fear for the ridge and the village
Whose peace and solitude will now be torn by
strife and sorrow.

(*She goes out. Enter Nyobi*)

## NYOBI

I was told she went this way.
Where is she now?
Thoni!
Don't leave me.
Thoni!
No answer?
Thoooni!
Oh my dream.

(*Rushes out*)


# SCENE III

(*Enter Remi and Omange talking*)

## OMANGE

That is the kind of thing we want in the country.
Yes, deal with tribalism with ruthless vigour.

REMI

There is no time for soft hearts.

OMANGE

Many of the elders felt guilty.

REMI

Yes, and turned their eyes away. But to-day's work is not enough. I mean to follow up this attack in my future political meetings. I want to inculcate in our people the need for self-help. We are the authors of our own destiny.

OMANGE

But the state must lead the way. The Africanist Party must first give back the Settlers' land to the people. Illiteracy ought to be abolished within a year. Otherwise they'll revert to tribalism and religion as a cure for their ills.

REMI

There is a limit to what the government can do.

OMANGE

There is a limit to patriotism and self-help schemes. (*Silence*) What, however, you have done to-day will be a big lesson to all our people in the country. Where did the girl go?

REMI

I don't know.

OMANGE

Let us spit on traditions. She was sitting in a corner. I saw her sneak out sometime during your speech.

REMI

(*Uneasily*) You see I told you she never loved me. She could not even wait to see what her man had to say.

OMANGE

Will you go back to Jane?
(*Before he answers the woman comes in and insolently throws
a letter to Remi* )

REMI

(*Scared*) Who gave it you?

WOMAN

She who was kind.
She who was true.
A tender sapling growing straight
Though surrounded with weed.

REMI

Who do you mean?

WOMAN

You are a leader!
Our leader indeed.
Know you not what you have done?
Flung insults at your own tribe,
Trampled mercilessly on wives everywhere?
You may praise yourself
(How you have succeeded at politics)
What of here?
What have you done to the lives of many?
To the hearts of many a man
Who looked up to you for guidance?

REMI

I am still in the dark
Who gave you the letter?
My mother?

## ACT III

*(Opens the letter)*

**WOMAN**

Your true wife.
The best woman the village had ever borne.
Many curses on you.
*(Goes out indignantly)*

**REMI**

Wait! Where has she gone to?

**OMANGE**

What is it? Why do you tremble so?
*(Remi can't speak. Points at the letter. Omange takes it, reads it, and looks at Remi)*

**OMANGE**

I don't understand. I told you she loved you.

**REMI**

Oh, my mother.
*(Rushes out)*

**OMANGE**

This outer frame can never tell what inner feelings are hidden here. I never thought Remi would be so shaken by a woman's love after all this victory. These village women! Why did she wait for all these years before she said *(waves the letter)* she loved him? What a heart? *(Looks at the letter. Then he starts laughing)* She cannot write properly. Ha! ha! ha! A mistake — all a mistake and it made him stay in the city for so long. And now after this reconcilation with his wife, who will be the loser? Jane. Poor, poor Jane!

(*Goes out laughing*)
(*Enter Nyobi followed by Pastor*)

NYOBI

I don't know where she went.

PASTOR

She will be found.

NYOBI

Education and big learning has taught him nothing.
I am an old woman,
Without learning or much wisdom,
Yet I know that what Remi has done is wrong.
Been so unfeeling to her
Who has always been true to him.

PASTOR

And where is he?
(*Enter Remi, followed by Omange*)

REMI

Mother! Pastor!

NYOBI

(*Coldly*) What do you want?
I thought you had gone back to the city.

REMI

Have you found her?

PASTOR

Who?

REMI

My wife.

NYOBI

Your wife indeed!

**PASTOR**

Why do you want her?
She has gone away.
(*All this time Remi looks agitated as if he fears something. Omange who does not know what he is fearing comes forward*)

**OMANGE**

She will come back. Whatever has happened do not blame yourself. It was a mistake. You did not know she loved you. Through that mistake, you have crushed tribalism and struck a blow for African Nationalism.

**REMI**

If I have achieved anything — No Omange, I have hurt my wife, I've hurt Thoni.

**NYOBI**

(*Changes now, full of a mother's concern*)
Pastor, you are a man of God. Help him, help my son.

**PASTOR**

I'll tell you what was wrong. You joined the Africanist Party and became lost in politics. You put all your trust in yourself and in man, not God —

**REMI**

Pastor, you and your religion never did anything for our people. It's only divided them and made them weak before the whiteman. (*Pastor goes out*)

**NYOBI**

What has come over him? (*To Omange*) You knew him in the city. Help him.

#### OMANGE

I think Remi is right. He has always been a true nationalist.

#### REMI

But Omange, what good has *my* nationalism done to people? What good to stand on a platform, control a crowd with a lift of the voice, silence them with a wave of the hand?

#### OMANGE

Great things have been achieved through that power: we now have our freedom—

#### REMI

And after? I have been a hermit . . . from my wife . . . from the people . . . I see now . . . a streak of light through the darkness . . . I have been too long away from their real thirst and hunger. (*Turning to Nyobi*) Mother, I know you know where she is. Don't hide her from me.

#### NYOBI

She was in the village. And then went away. I could not follow her. She will be found.

#### REMI

What have I done? What have I done?

(*Drums beat in slow rhythm. A procession of elders and women led by the leader file onto the stage. Four men carry Thoni's body on a stretcher. They put it down and step to the side. The pastor steps forward*)

#### PASTOR

Stand you not near her.
Though she took her own life,
She was holy,
She was of God.

# ACT III

*(Kneeling beside her — broken)*
And she is gone now,
Gone from me and my heart,
With her words of love
Still ringing in my heart.
Dear Remi — I loved you all my life.
Oh, what have I done.
Thoni, what have I done?
I wish you had sent the letter earlier.
But I never gave you a chance,
Nor even tried to understand you.
I came back to break Tribe and Custom,
Instead, I've broken you and me.

# THE AFRICAN WRITERS SERIES

The book you have been reading is part of Heinemann's long-established series of African fiction. Details of some of the other titles are given below, but for a catalogue giving information on all the titles in this series and the Caribbean Writers Series write to: Heinemann Educational Publishers, Halley Court, Jordan Hill, Oxford OX2 8EJ; United States customers should write to: Heinemann, 361 Hanover Street, Portsmouth, NH 03801-3912, USA.

## NGŪGĪ
### Matigari

This is a moral fable telling the story of a freedom fighter and his quest for Truth and Justice. Set in the political dawn of a post-independence Kenya.
'Clear, subtle, mischievous passionate novel.' *Sunday Times*

### Devil on the Cross

Written secretly in prison, on lavatory paper, while the author was detained without trial, this novel is a powerful critique of modern Kenya.

### A Grain of Wheat

'With Mr Ngũgĩ, history is living tissue. He writes with poise from deep reserves, and the book adds cubits to his already considerable stature.' *The Guardian*

### Petals of Blood

A compelling novel about the tragedy of corrupting power, set in post-independence Kenya.
'. . . Ngũgĩ writes with passion about every form, shape and colour which power can take.' *Sunday Times*

## Weep Not, Child

This powerful, moving story about the effects of the Mau Mau war on the lives of ordinary men and women in Kenya, is one of the best-known of Ngũgĩ's works. 'This story is a skilful work of art.' *Times Literary Supplement*


## The River Between

'A sensitive novel about the Gikuyu in the melting pot that sometimes touches the grandeur of tap-root simplicity.' *The Guardian*


## STEVE BIKO
### I Write What I Like

'An impressive tribute to the depth and range of his thought, covering such diverse issues as the basic philosophy of black consciousness, Bantustans, African culture, the institutional church, and Western involvement in apartheid.' *The Catholic Herald*


## NELSON MANDELA
### No Easy Walk to Freedom

A collection of the articles, speeches, letters and trials of the most important figure in the South African liberation struggle.


## OLIVER TAMBO
### Preparing for Power – Oliver Tambo Speaks

This selection of speeches, interviews and letters offers a unique insight into the ANC President's views on the history of the freedom struggle within South Africa and, of even greater importance, his vision for the future.

## DORIS LESSING
### The Grass is Singing

The classic murder story of the Rhodesian farmer's wife and her houseboy.

## NADINE GORDIMER
### Some Monday for Sure

Nadine Gordimer has used these stories from her five collections to tell of the daily frustrations and contradictions of life in South African society.

## AMECHI AKWANYA
### Orimili

Set in a complex Nigerian community that's at the point of irrevocable change, this is the story of a man's struggle to be accepted in the company of his town's elders.

## EARL McKENZIE
### A Boy Named Ossie

Ossie, a young Jamaican boy, is the tool through which Earl McKenzie expertly portrays the reality of life in rural Jamaica; its humour, warmth and ambitions, as well as its terrors and tribulations.

'Zimbabwe has fine black writers and Shimmer Chinodya is one of the best. *Harvest of Thorns* brilliantly pictures the transition between the old white dominated Southern Rhodesia, through the Bush War, to the new black regime. It is a brave book, a good strong story, and it is often very funny. People who know the country will salute its honesty, but I hope newcomers to African writing will give this book a try. They won't be disappointed.'
*Doris Lessing*

## CHINUA ACHEBE
### Things Fall Apart

This, the first title in the African Writers Series, describes how a man in the Obi tribe of South Africa became exiled from the tribe and returned only to be forced to commit suicide to escape the results of his rash courage against the white man.